Animal Self-Defence

Written by Jo Windsor

T0350586

Contents

Introduction

Day-to-day life can be very dangerous for lots of animals. They might have to **defend** themselves against other animals that want to attack them, or to kill them for food.

A starling

A harvest mouse

A salmon

A hare

Ways of defence

Different animals choose different ways to defend themselves. Some animals hide, some run away, and some pretend to be dead. There are even some animals that choose to attack.

Here are some of the main ways that animals defend themselves.

A ruffled grouse

Camouflage

An animal that is **camouflaged** looks like its surroundings or other animals. There are lots of ways an animal can be camouflaged.

Colour

If an animal has a bright colour, this can tell a **predator** to stay away because it might not taste very nice!

A blue poison dart frog

Safety in numbers

This type of defence needs lots of animals. Large groups of animals, fish, birds and insects can work together to protect themselves.

A herd of impala

Attack or threat

Some animals squirt poison at their attacker. Other animals make themselves look threatening.

A sea urchin

What am I?

A camouflaged animal is unlikely to be attacked because the predator cannot see it easily. Some animals are born camouflaged. Others can change the way they look.

There are different sorts of camouflage.

The Kalahari ground is the same colour as the desert sand gecko

Shades

Some animals are a darker shade of colour on the upper part of their body, and a lighter shade underneath. When an animal blends in with the colour of the ground, a predator cannot easily spot it from above.

A herd of plains zebras

Stripes

Other animals depend on patterns of colour. A herd of zebras confuses predators. Their stripes blend together, making it difficult for a predator to pick out an individual zebra to chase.

Now you see me ...
now you don't

Some animals **mimic** something else that a predator thinks isn't very tasty. For example, the sphinx moth can make itself look exactly like the bark of a tree.

A sphinx moth

A leaf insect

Leaf and stick insects have the colour and shape to make them look like the leaf or stick they are clinging onto.

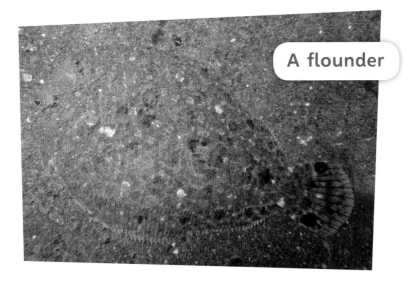

A flounder

Flounders change their colour to match their background. They flick sand over their bodies, too, so that they can hide themselves on the seabed.

It's safer at night

The eggs of green sea turtles always hatch at night. The **hatchlings** are all born at the same time on the same night, and then they rush down the beach to the sea. They do this at night so that gulls and other predators are less likely to be around to catch and eat them.

An adult Manx shearwater gull in its burrow

Manx shearwater gulls lay their eggs in **burrows**. The adults only go to their burrows at night so that they are less likely to be seen by predators.

Green sea turtle hatchlings heading for the sea

It's a slow life

Some animals are slow-moving, or **immobile**. They have developed hard shells or spines for protection. These animals sit tight, hiding or covering their **vulnerable** parts.

A snail

A hawksbill turtle

When they are threatened, turtles, snails, clams and mussels pull the soft parts of their bodies into their shells.

A hedgehog

Hedgehogs and porcupine fish make their spines stand up straight, and roll into a ball for extra protection.

A flash of colour

A sudden flash of colour on a prey's body can confuse a predator. The predator might then go for a less vulnerable part of its prey's body, or it might simply go away.

An underwing moth

The bright hind wings of underwing moths are covered by camouflaged front wings. When a predator comes near, the moth flashes its hind wings to frighten the predator away.

Hawk moths have large spots of colour on their hind wings. Predators are scared off because the spots look like large eyes.

A hawk moth

Running and jumping

Sometimes, running is the best thing to do!
Prairie dogs and meerkats usually stay close
to their burrows, so they don't have far to run
when one of the group gives the alarm call
that a predator is nearby.

A meerkat running for cover

Other animals try to **outrun** their attacker.
When they run from foxes, hares run in a zigzag
pattern, hoping that this will slow the fox down.

Running zigzag helps a snowshoe hare to outrun a mountain lion

Antelopes are very fast, and **agile**, too. As they run, they often spring from the ground with all four feet in the air. This may be a signal to the attacker to chase an animal that is less fit!

An antelope in mid air

All puffed up!

Bullfrogs and toads are clever. When they are trapped, they put on an act to frighten off their attacker. They swallow air to puff themselves up so that they look much bigger than normal.

An African giant bull frog

Pufferfish have spines, but they are vulnerable because they swim slowly. They can escape a predator by swallowing masses of water into their elastic tummies, and turning themselves into huge, spiky balls.

A spotted pufferfish

Did I leave something behind?

Lizards are extraordinary when predators threaten them, or attack them by the tail. They have special parts in the **vertebrae** of their tails which allow them to **shed** the tail and run away. A new tail does grow, although it's not quite as good as the old one!

A lizard can shed its tail when it needs to

Painful and pongy

Some insects have poisons stored in their bodies which they squirt onto their attacker – sometimes at up to 500 squirts a second! The bombardier beetle sprays boiling hot liquid poison at a predator from special **glands** in the tip of its **abdomen**.

tip of the abdomen

A bombardier beetle

Bear cubs have to learn that skunks are not easy prey!

Skunks have very poor eyesight, so they are particularly vulnerable to attack. Their trick is to spray a foul-smelling liquid called musk at predators – and this comes out of their bottom!

All together now

Many animals work **co-operatively** to defend themselves.

In Africa, herds of eland are hunted by spotted hyenas. The eland often remain safe because they work together. The cows with calves stay well back, and the cows without calves face their attackers, using their horns and hooves to defend themselves.

A herd of eland

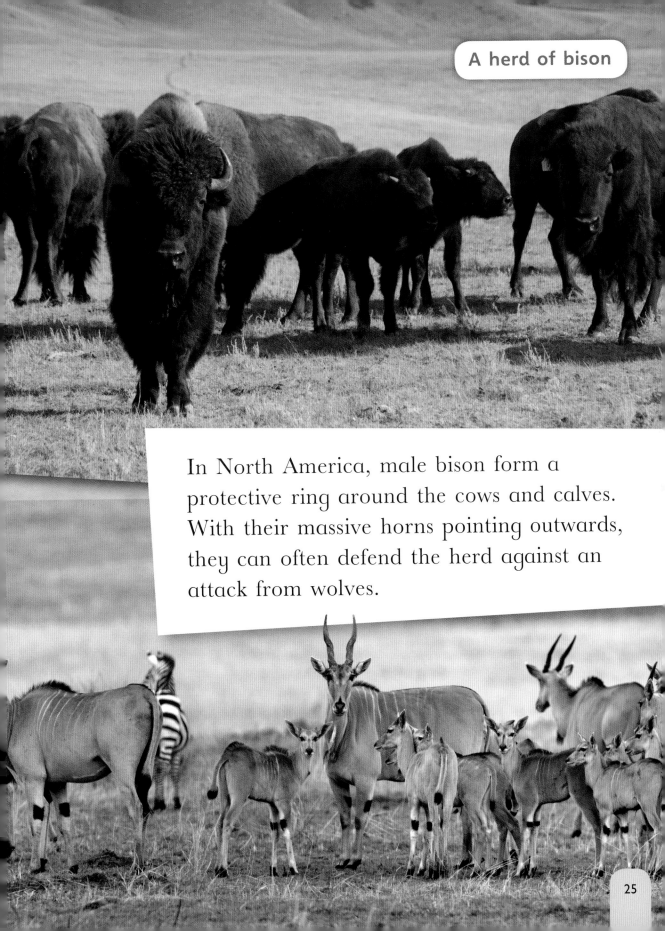

A herd of bison

In North America, male bison form a protective ring around the cows and calves. With their massive horns pointing outwards, they can often defend the herd against an attack from wolves.

Flocks and colonies

Very large groups of birds and insects are able to work co-operatively.

At **dusk**, thousands of starlings come together in a huge flock, called a murmuration. The birds twist and turn at great speed. They do this to protect themselves from hawks and falcons. The birds keep changing places, as it is more dangerous on the edge of the flock than in the middle.

A murmuration of starlings

In some leaf cutter ant **colonies**, large worker ants carry pieces of leaves back to the nest as food for the **fungi** gardens that they grow. Smaller ants go with them to fight off the wasps which try to attack and eat the worker ants.

Leaf cutter ants collecting leaves

Playing possum

Beetles, spiders and snakes stay still, sometimes just for a few minutes, sometimes for hours, until the predator gets bored. Hog-nosed snakes play dead by rolling onto their backs with their mouth open.

An eastern hog-nosed snake 'playing dead'

Possums escape attack by foaming at the mouth and appearing to be dead, or at least very sick. This puts off a predator.

Quiz

1 Why is a camouflaged animal not likely to be attacked?
  a Because a predator can't see it properly.
  b Because it gets very cross if it is disturbed.
  c Because predators can't be bothered to attack it.

2 What does a flatfish do to hide itself on the seabed?
  a It digs a hole.
  b It hides under a rock.
  c It flips sand over itself.

3 How do male bison protect their herd?
  a They stay with the calves while the mothers chase the attackers.
  b They lead the herd into a pool and stand in it.
  c They form a protective circle around the herd.

4 What is the word that describes a flock of starlings flying at dusk?
  a chatter
  b murmuration
  c gossip

Answers on page 31

Glossary

abdomen	back part of an insect's body
agile	quick-moving
burrows	holes dug in earth by some animals and birds
camouflaged	disguised
colonies	groups of same species living together
co-operatively	together
defend	protect
dusk	evening, when it is beginning to get dark
fungi	mushrooms and toadstools
glands	parts of the body that produce chemicals
hatchlings	newborn animals hatched from eggs
immobile	not moving
mimic	copy, look like
outrun	run faster or further than
predator	animal that hunts other animals
shed	get rid of
vertebrae	bones that make up the spine
vulnerable	likely to be injured

Index